SOCIAL EUROPE

VOLUME 3

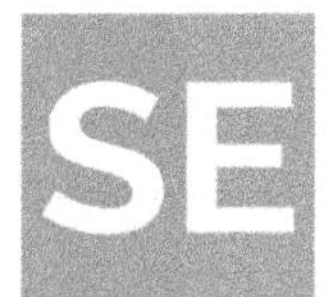

ISBN paperback: 978-3-948314-13-2

ISBN ebook: 978-3-948314-11-8

Copyright © 2020 by Social Europe Publishing

Berlin, Germany

CONTENTS

FOREWORD

ROBIN WILSON

These have been, in human terms, desperate times for Europe —of countless individual tragedies, of suffering and bereavement, with a depression looming on a scale as nothing since the 1930s.

Yet it is precisely in such times that solidarity turns from a slogan into an imperative—we might call it 'social closing'—which can uplift the most vulnerable and secure the most fearful. It is in such times that politics, as the pursuit of public purpose for collective ends, can and must offer a credible message of hope that there are better times ahead—there being plenty in the wings keen to exploit the Covid-19 shock for divisive, power-hungry ends.

To achieve that public purpose, diverse ideas have to come together and be framed by a common narrative, gelled by a commitment to values which are universal and enlightenment-based. The progressive values of the liberal-socialist tradition

—of liberty, equality and solidarity—now given a feminist inflection and complemented by an ecological value of sustainability, provide invaluable glue for a post-crisis recovery which is not a return to 'business as usual'.

That very phrase encapsulated the decades of dogmatic devotion to deregulated markets, which delegitimised civic action and democratic politics. Yet the new paradigm emerging cloudily from the searing experience of the pandemic is already clearly foregrounding not the hedonic treadmill of individual acquisitiveness but the spontaneous embrace of social responsibility.

In this volume of material collected from *Social Europe* over the period since the beginning of 2020, we draw together just some of the rich profusion of ideas presented on the site in recent months, at a time when public opinion and the sense of possibility have never seemed more fluid in living memory. In a way, in these thousands and thousands of words our contributors all pose, and attempt variously to answer, the question: now what?

They show how phrases such as 'green new deal' and 'just transition' are rapidly entering the popular lexicon, how public goods such as health and clean air are suddenly being revalorised over private commodities, how precarious 'essential workers' are dramatically being accorded more esteem than high-rolling *rentiers*. It is thus that what appears on *Social Europe* today seeks to help set the agenda for the Europe of tomorrow.

This must be a Europe revitalised by that new progressive paradigm and so able to rise, in unity of purpose, above the old nationalistic reflexes which still tug from the past. All the evidence is that Europe's citizens—scarred by a postwar episode only exceeded by the trauma of the wars of the Yugoslav succession—demand no less. It is the least the unnumbered bereaved deserve.

Robin Wilson

acting editor-in-chief, *Social Europe*

ONE

THE TRIUMPH OF INJUSTICE

A CONVERSATION WITH GABRIEL ZUCMAN

Earlier this year, as editor-in-chief of *Social Europe* Henning Meyer talked to the US inequality expert Gabriel Zucman about the sources of the marked rise of in-country inequality in recent decades and what can be done to reverse it. Zucman is professor of economics at the University of California at Berkeley, director of the Stone Centre on Wealth and Inequality there and co-author with Emmanuel Saez of *The Triumph of Injustice: How the Rich Dodge Taxes and How to Make them Pay.*

Meyer: Gabriel Zucman, thank you very much indeed for taking the time to talk to me about the topic of your most recent book. What would you say is the situation currently in western economies when it comes to the distribution of wealth and income?

Zucman: There is a discontent in many parts of the western

world with the rise of inequality, which is happening in most developed countries, although at different speed. In 1980 the top 1 per cent's income share was 10 per cent in the US and in western Europe. Today it's 20 per cent in the US, 12 per cent in western Europe, so inequality has increased in both cases but more in the US than in Europe.

What do you think are the key drivers of this drive towards higher inequality?

There are two theses. There is one view which says this is due to globalisation and technological change, which has made workers less productive, and there's another view which says this is mostly due to policies and changes in public policies.

The fact that inequality has increased everywhere but quite differently—especially it has increased much more in the US —is more consistent with the view that the main driver is policy changes, that these changes have been particularly extreme in the US.

Think about financial deregulation. Think about the collapse in the minimum wage, the decline in the power of unions, the huge changes in taxation, in tax progressivity. The US used to have the most progressive tax system in the world. It has changed in the post-World War II decades. It has changed dramatically since the 1980s. Some of these changes have also happened in Europe but to a slightly less extreme degree— hence the difference in the rise of inequality. Policies are the key driver.

Because, if the first thesis were true, you would expect the application of technology to be very similar across the board—but the results are very different.

Yes, of course. If technology and globalisation in itself—international trade—was the key driver, we should see inequality increase pretty much everywhere at the same pace. In Europe people have computers, as well, and just like in the US, and they trade a lot with emerging economies, with China —even more, actually, than the US—but we don't see this inequality rising exactly the same way everywhere.

What role do the different political economies, rather than the policies, play—the institutional setup, how the economies are constituted?

Behind these big changes in policies, there is, of course, a change in politics, and in ideology and the triumph, if you want, of free-market ideas and small-government ideas—what people sometimes call 'neoliberalism' or 'market fundamental-ism', the idea that markets are always the best way to organise economic and social activity. These ideas have been very powerful for many years, for many decades.
At the same time, we see today that the neoliberal model has clear limits. The rise of inequality is one. The problem with global warming is the other one—environmental degradation —and so there is a demand for an alternative model.

As an economist, where would you draw the line?

**Where are markets the right mechanism to effi-
ciently distribute scarce resources, and where do
other factors, like providing public goods and other
ideas, play a significant role?**

It's not for economists to say. It's for the public to decide about
what should be provided by governments, by the community
rather than by the market. There is a consensus in many countries, and certainly in Europe, that healthcare, education—
including early childhood education, childcare—are better
provided by the community than by the market. Not only
more efficiently but also in a more inclusive manner, because
healthcare is very costly, childcare is very costly, which means
that if you only rely on private provision, with no public subsi-
dies, then you exclude lots of people from these essential
services.

But, fundamentally, it's for people to decide through democratic deliberation and the vote. It's not for economists to say
'This should be, probably, a better market / It should be, probably, a better government.' This is a key political question,
where the frontier should be put. Nobody has the truth, a
definitive answer to that question, which can only be obtained
through the broadest democratic discussion.

**So it's about an estimation of the upsides and the
downsides. Then it's a political deliberation and the
outcome of a political system, with democratic legitimacy, that needs to draw the line?**

Exactly, and the same thing for taxation. It's not for economists to say 'The top tax grade for the wealthiest individuals should be X or Y' or 'The level of the tax-to-GDP ratio should be 30 per cent or 50 per cent or 70 per cent'—not at all. Again, it has to be the outcome of a democratic debate, and debates in Parliament, and the broadest public discussion and confrontation of ideas possible.

But, as you know, quite a few economists actually do that and say, for instance, 'Debt-to-GDP ratio of 90 per cent—that's where the dynamics change.' So you don't see any iron laws where empirical evidence really points to different dynamics but it's a purely political decision?

No public-policy question can be conclusively settled by economic research or research in the social sciences. The theories that we construct are all provisory and imperfect, and there is never the truth. Nobody has the truth on these important questions, but we contribute collectively to a more informed debate, or we can contribute.

That's why it's perfectly legitimate for economists to intervene in the public debate, to talk about new ideas—sometimes to defend new ideas—but none of them can pretend to have a definitive answer, because none of them has a definitive answer.

As you mentioned, but quite a few economists often do not, there are a lot of other contributing factors

that are part of the political decision-making process that need to be taken into account, that are not involved in any sort of academic research, whether it's in economics or any other social sciences.

Yes. economics in itself cannot provide the answers. But I think we economists can be useful in several ways. For instance, one is contributing to a more informed democratic debate by providing facts about, for instance, how inequality has evolved, who pays what in taxes, how progressive a tax system really is.

When it comes to taxes, another way that we can be useful is by being a bit like plumbers. Esther Duflo has a famous article, 'The economist as a plumber'. It's a metaphor that works really well for taxation. If there is a popular democratic demand for a more progressive tax system, we economists who work on taxation, we can help design taxes that will work, that will address this demand for redistribution.

We can help explain how it's possible to tax better multinational companies, to tax very wealthy individuals in a globalised world, how it's possible to reconcile globalisation with progressive taxation—not to substitute ourselves for the public debate but, if there is this democratic will, we can help the world and public policies work a bit better.

Let's get to the topic of your most recent book—how to tax the rich or how the rich avoid paying their fair share of taxes, which is a prerequisite of the distrib-

ution of wealth and income we already mentioned. What do you think are the biggest problems?

The key problem is that there has been a triumph of what we call 'tax injustice'. What is tax injustice? It's a process by which the big winners from globalisation—multinational companies and their shareholders—have seen their taxes fall while at the same time the economic actors who have not benefited a lot from globalisation, like small businesses, or retirees or low-wage workers, have seen their taxes increase.

To put it differently, it's the combination of two phenomena. One is the rise of inequality on one hand. The other is the decline of tax progressivity on the other hand. What is behind the decline in tax progressivity? Some of this is due to ideological change—to the triumph of the idea that, by taxing the wealthy less, you will have growth trickling down to the rest of the population—but that's not fundamental.

Maybe what is more fundamental is that policy-makers from both left and right have become convinced, often sincerely, that in a globalised world you can't tax the more mobile tax bases, like these big multinational firms or these very wealthy individuals. If you do so, they will move abroad. They will shift profits to tax havens. They will expatriate. They will hide assets. They will conceal wealth. They will use this tax-optimisation industry that has developed.

We wrote the book *The Triumph of Injustice* to explain why this view not only is dangerous but also is wrong. It's dangerous because globalisation is unlikely to be a sustainable process if it means ever-lower taxes for its main winners and higher taxes for those who don't benefit a lot from it. It's not sustainable politically or economically but, more importantly, it's wrong because there are concrete ways to reconcile globalisation and progressive taxation.

In the book we make concrete proposals, for instance for collecting what we call the 'tax deficit' of multinational companies and for taxing people with a lot of wealth—who today have a low effective tax rate—by reinventing wealth taxation for the 21st century. It's a message of hope. We can, if we choose, have a progressive tax system, potentially high capital taxation, even in the era of globalisation.

So the overall evidence seems to be that the tax quota has remained largely constant but the tax burden has shifted from the winners—who claim 'We are mobile; if you tax us as you used to, we'll just go away'—to the immobile subjects.

Yes. Two illustrations: one is the US and the other is going to be more about Europe. If you look at the US today, when you take into account all taxes at all levels of government, each group of the population, the working class, the middle class, the upper middle class, pays around 28 per cent of its income in taxes, with one—one and only one—exception, which is billionaires, who in 2018 paid only 23 per cent of their income in taxes. To put it differently, the US tax system is like a giant flat tax that becomes regressive at the very top end, with billionaires paying less as a portion of their income than their secretaries, basically.

In Europe there is pretty much the same phenomenon. For instance, in a country like France, it's also the case that the tax system becomes regressive at the top, that effective tax rates decline below the average effective tax rate when you enter the top 0.1 per cent. The only difference is just that the tax uptake is higher. In the US it's 28 per cent for most of the population, then falling to 23 per cent. In a country like France, it would be 20 points more—48 per cent falling to 43 per cent—but the same process is true in France.

In many ways, the underlying forces that have led to this regressive tax system are even stronger in the European Union, where you have tax competition that is very severe, with the number of tax havens within the EU offering very low tax rates, competing with other countries, where you've seen a number of countries offering special tax regimes for mobile tax bases. For instance, researchers or high-wage earners or the wealthy in Denmark can get lower tax rates in Greece. Within Italy and Portugal, we now have a special tax regime to attract retirees.

These forces of tax competition have been very strong, and forces of tax evasion as well—with, for a very long time, massive concealment of wealth in tax havens like Switzerland, Luxembourg and so on. That's the driving force behind the decline in tax progressivity.

There is a competition in terms, for instance, of the

headline corporate-tax rate, but barely any company pays the headline tax anyway. Isn't it sometimes smoke and mirrors when you have a political haggle over the actual tax rate?

Yes, even in a tax haven like Ireland that has a low statutory tax rate of 12.5 per cent, the effective tax rate—at least for foreign multinationals—is much lower than that: it's around 5 per cent. There is a lot of opacity about the tax rates that this and that company get, with special tax deals that were granted to specific firms. That is being investigated by the European Commission.

There is this problem, and there is a feeling of hopelessness in the EU because for tax matters the rule for the EU is unanimity. So, there is no tax harmonisation: no common tax policy is possible unless the 27 member states agree on that common tax policy, which in practice is equivalent to saying that there will never be any tax policy, because some countries benefit a lot from the *status quo* and from the current race to the bottom.

That's why one idea that we push in the book is the somewhat paradoxical idea that in practice the way to reach an international agreement or EU-wide co-ordination is by having countries, at least initially, taking unilateral action— saying 'We are going to start collecting the tax deficit of multi-national firms.'

So, Germany, let's say, could say 'Starting January 1st 2021, for each firm we are going to compute their tax deficit'—meaning the difference between what they pay in taxes today and what they would pay if they were taxed at a rate of 25 per cent, on a country-by-country basis—'then we, Germany, are going to collect part of that tax deficit.' For a firm that makes 20 per cent of its global sales in Germany, Germany could say 'We are going to collect 20 per cent of the tax deficit.'

If a country like Germany—or a small coalition of countries, like Germany and France or France and Belgium—starts doing this and demonstrates that in practice it is possible to tax more the big multinational firms that don't pay a lot in taxes today, then very quickly you will see other countries doing the same, saying 'Look, there is money on the table. There is a tax deficit in that some countries choose not to collect taxes, but we can collect the taxes that they choose not to collect. We can act as tax collectors of last resort.'
So you see how very quickly you can get a form of tax harmonisation where all countries, in fact, collect the tax deficit. In effect, the tax rate becomes 25 per cent pretty much everywhere because, in a world where some countries act as tax collector of last resort, there wouldn't be any incentive any more for firms to book earnings in tax havens—because low tax rates in Ireland would be offset by higher tax payments in Germany or in France.

There wouldn't be an incentive any more for tax havens to offer a low tax rate in the first place, and you would see Ireland and Bermuda increase their tax rate. So we would move from the current race to the bottom to a race to the top. It can happen relatively quickly, once at least one or two countries pave the way for this kind of shift in global behaviour.

Some of this effective minimum taxation is being pushed in the OECD framework. The German policy discussion is around creating something like this, especially in the OECD framework and if not at least within the European Union. How do you evaluate these recent attempts?

The current discussion, as with the OECD about minimum taxation, is clearly going in the right direction. For a long time, the OECD was only talking about the definition of the tax base. But if you have a perfectly defined tax base and then you apply a rate of 5 per cent, 2 per cent and 0 per cent eventually, it's a big waste of time. So it's good to finally talk about minimum taxation.

Of course, the question is what is going to be the minimum tax rate. If it is just to pick the lowest tax rate among G20 countries, you've not really made any progress. If the minimum tax rate becomes something like 20 per cent, 25 per cent, then we'll really change things. So, a lot will depend on what is the tax rate that's agreed upon.

I want to stress that in the system we describe in the book—collecting the tax deficit of multinational companies—by its construction, if Germany did it, it would gain tax revenue. The idea is to let countries do what they do today—change nothing. Let them have their corporate tax rate and the current system. Simply put, if some companies have a tax deficit—that is, they have a less than 25 per cent effective tax rate—there must be at least one country that steps in and says 'We are going to collect part of that tax deficit.'

Any country that does that is going to only increase its tax collection. For the companies that are already paying 25 per cent or more, country by country, they have no tax deficit. For them nothing changes. It's only for the corporations that have less than 25 per cent country-by-country tax rate that taxes will increase. This would increase tax collection in any country.

One of the problems I hear in these discussions is that this would flip the system because it's no longer you tax at the place of production but, effectively, tax at the place of sale. Is that one of the difficulties of implementing this?

No, again the idea is just to say any country should do whatever it does today or whatever it wants to do. For some countries, it makes sense to have taxes based on the location of production. Let them do whatever they want, but in the current system there is no guardrail. If a company has been able to shift profits to tax havens and to book billions in zero-tax bases—Google, for instance, in 2018 made $20bn in revenue in Bermuda, so there is a tax deficit—this means that no country taxes these profits in Bermuda.

The only idea that we are putting forward in the book—and it's a new idea but it's a simple idea—is just to say some countries have to step in and say 'Look, it's the right of Bermuda to choose a 0 per cent tax rate. It's the right of Ireland to choose 12.5 per cent, or in practice 5 per cent. But we—Germany, or France or Belgium—consider that the normal rate is 25 per cent. If you want to have access to our market and you have a tax deficit related to this norm of 25 per cent, you will have to pay an extra tax in Germany, in France or in Belgium.'

You mentioned that this is a nice way to avoid the collective-action problem in these sorts of issues—but, at the same time, the more countries which would adopt such a policy at the same time, the more effective it would be. Do you see any chance that at least some of the leading European countries could come together?

I am very optimistic because once one country does that and demonstrates they have been able to increase tax collection by collecting part of the tax deficit of Google or Apple or the French multinationals, or whatever, then other countries will say 'That's incredible. There is money on the table here to grab. France is grabbing part of it, but why don't we do it as well?'

You will see a process starting like that where all countries start collecting part of the tax deficit, until there is no tax deficit anymore and all corporations pay at least 25 per cent, country by country. There you go—you harmonised corporate tax rates.

This is basically how you could tax corporations, but what about wealthy individuals?

Wealthy individuals is a problem that also has a solution. In the debate about wealth taxation in Europe, one recurring idea is that it's impossible to tax the super-rich because, if we do it on our own, then they will expatriate—they will move to Switzerland or to low-tax places that don't have a wealth tax.

The answer is pretty simple. The answer is to say countries should tax expatriates for at least a few years. So let's say you've made a huge fortune in Germany, you've become a billionaire. It's good for you, it's great, but you've become a billionaire, in part, thanks to German infrastructure and German workers who've been trained by German teachers. All German taxpayers have helped pay for these things through their taxes. There is no natural right to expatriate, to move to a tax haven once you've become a billionaire and immediately stop paying anything to Germany. It doesn't make sense.

The US is the polar case. In the US, if you are a US national —you are a citizen—you have to pay taxes, no matter where you live. Taxes follow you for the rest of your life. Maybe it's too extreme, but the polar opposite, which is what European countries are doing today—as soon as you move on January 1st of the next year, you don't have to pay anything any more to your home country—is too extreme as well.

So the solution that I defend is to reach a middle ground that says 'If you have been a tax resident—let's say in Germany—

for 20 years or 30 years and you move abroad, you still have to pay taxes in Germany for, maybe, 5, 10 years,' depending on the number of years that you've been a tax resident in Germany. Like that, we can reduce dramatically the problem of tax competition between countries, and the risk of expatriation.

How would you deal with the potential double taxation, say if you then move to Switzerland and they tax as well?

You could give credits. What Germany would say is, 'You still have to pay taxes in Germany, with credit given for foreign taxes,' so, if you move to a country that also has a wealth tax, which is the same as the German wealth tax, you wouldn't have anything to pay in Germany.

It's just like it works in the US right now if you are a US citizen: you move to France, you have to pay taxes in France— there is basically no extra in the US. But if you move to the Cayman Islands, there is no tax in the Cayman Islands and you have to pay extra taxes in the US.

So, basically linking taxation to citizenship, to a large extent, then, as well.

Not necessarily citizenship but linking taxation to where you've built your wealth, for the purpose of the wealth tax. If you become a billionaire by being a tax burden in Germany for 30 years, you owe something to the German community, okay?

So, it's legitimate for Germany to say 'You're going to have to pay taxes for a few extra years in Germany.'

So, to residency, effectively?

Yes, to residency, to where you've made your worth.

If we come now to the political solutions, if you were a policy-maker, where would you start? What would be your top three policy recommendations—maybe for a nation state, as well as for the European Union?

Collecting the tax deficits of multinationals is one, so to demonstrate very clearly that it's possible to reconcile globalisation and capital taxation, and to make the big winners from globalisation contribute more. This would help reconcile the working class and the middle class with globalisation and with European integration, showing 'Look, we can tax these big winners,' which means that we can also cut taxes for the working class and the middle class—because in the European Union, in many countries, the tax-to-GDP ratio is already pretty high. The point is not to increase, necessarily, tax collection. The US is different, but in many European countries you can imagine just to collect more taxes on some actors and to cut taxes on the rest of the population.

The wealth tax is the same logic—to reintroduce a modern wealth tax that draws the lessons from the long European experience with wealth taxation, that dates back to the 19th century and that had limitations. There was no serious attempt at taxing expatriates. There was a lot of tax evasion. The wealth taxes were archaic, with no pre-populated wealth-tax returns, so people just had to self-declare their wealth, with lots of lobbying to introduce exemption and adaptations over time.

I would recreate a wealth tax that brought the lessons from all of this, which means, maybe, starting a bit higher in the wealth distribution. The European wealth taxes started around $1 million. Today what is proposed in the US by Elizabeth Warren or Bernie Sanders is wealth taxes that start at around €30 million in net wealth, but in exchange for that to have really broad taxes on all assets above 30 million--no deduction, no exemption.

The third thing is, of course, environmental taxes, carbon taxes, and maybe potentially progressive carbon taxes if we found good ways to measure emissions at the individual level —that is something that is totally doable.

To me, these are important reforms to illustrate the idea that 'Look, we can combine a thriving market economy, globalisation, European integration, with safeguarding the climate, the planet, on one hand, and making sure that the gains from globalisation are spread out, are equally distributed, rather than concentrated in just a few hands.'

TWO

A JUST TRANSITION WITH CLIMATE AND SOCIAL AMBITION

TERESA RIBERA

We find ourselves immersed in an unprecedented climate emergency, which is putting the current model of development at risk, increasing inequality and affecting especially the most vulnerable. Governments have to lead this transformation and we have to carry it out within the timescales that science sets for us and with the profundity that is necessary—no less.

This is not time to be lukewarm. Either we drastically reduce emissions or the future will be extremely hard for the most vulnerable on the planet and we will destroy a 'natural capital' that does not belong only to us but also the generations to come.

Collective talent

In this world of accelerating climate change, we need to be able to act in a manner that is innovative, strong and coherent.

We need to pay attention to the direction of the changes in order to anticipate them, to generate proposals that meet the scale of the challenges and to multiply and expand our collective talent.

The only way to avoid climate chaos is if the transformation is taken on as a cohesive, robust proposition—a plan in which everyone has a role to play, in which no one is left behind. Ambition in climate commitments must go hand in hand with ambition in social guarantees, so that the changes that occur do not negatively affect those who have the least, but rather become a catalyst for opportunities precisely for them.

The objectives of the Paris agreement are fundamental to guarantee justice and equity in all societies, particularly in the poorest societies and in the least-favoured strata in all countries. Without accelerated climate action, a just transition cannot be realised.

However, accelerating mitigation policies without deep reflection on who will be the winners and losers of the transition to fully decarbonised economies will not engender the support and confidence of populations and communities who feel threatened by the very important change we have to undertake. Although the benefits far outweigh the adverse effects, attention must also be paid to these.

We have to move forward on climate policies yet while analysing well the economic contexts in which they must be implemented. In many countries, including many European countries, climate policies now have to be implemented in some national contexts where progress in social indicators is arrested or in retreat, where the indicators of inequality do not stop rising. Social indicators going in reverse debilitate in a profound way our ability to undertake transformations of all kinds.

More and better jobs

Employment is one of the fundamental elements to consider, because the incomes of families and their ability to prosper depend on its realisation and its quality. Climate action has to be a vector of creating more and better jobs and it must pay attention to the job losses which some of the associated changes can bring in train. In a country such as Spain, where unemployment levels remain high, this fact has been a key element of our action as a government.

That is why at the national level we have been developing a battery of responses to ensure that in Spain the transition to a decarbonised economy is just. Last year we presented the Strategic Framework for Energy and Climate, focused on facilitating the modernisation of the economy towards a sustainable and competitive model.

This is about different elements designed together so that Spain relies on a solid and stable strategic framework for the decarbonisation of its economy:

- a draft Climate Change and Energy Transition law, which aims for emissions neutrality in 2050;
- an Integrated National Energy and Climate Plan 2021-2030, much in line with a goal for the European

> Union of reduction of emissions by close to 55 per cent, with the current rules for sharing out, and

- an accompanying strategy of support and just transition, to ensure that individuals and regions make the most of the opportunities of this transition, so that no one is left behind.

Finally, together with the climate and energy strategic framework, we approved an Energy Poverty Strategy to protect vulnerable consumers. And elaboration of a long-term decarbonisation strategy—a document expected to be delivered to the European Commission in the short term and whose central objective is for Spain to achieve climate neutrality by 2050—is well advanced.

Mobilising investment

We set ambitious goals from a climate point of view because we know they will create significant opportunities for the country. The Integrated National Energy and Climate Plan will mobilise more than €230 billion over the next decade from private, public and mixed investment and boost growth in growth domestic product against a scenario without such a plan.

It will also allow Spain to reduce its energy dependence and to improve its trade balance by around €70 billion between 2020 and 2030. And it will allow the not inconsiderable reduction, by around 25 per cent, of the number of premature deaths caused by air pollution, compared with a no-plan scenario.

Finally, it will have a positive effect on employment, as approximately 250,000 to 350,000 jobs will be created over the next decade, especially in manufacturing and construction, in a country such as Spain which needs its economy to generate more and better jobs.

We understand however that for the social and employment gains to be optimised, measures must be proposed among the different administrations—within the government (Industry, Labour, Agriculture, Economy, Finance, Education), between the different levels of the administration in Spain, from the local to the state, and through social dialogue, with employers, trade-union organisations and other social actors—to seek the most appropriate solutions.

In this way, our proposal for just transition includes sectoral policies for optimising the results, in terms of employment, of the ecological transition of the economy as the Green New Deal at European level aims to do as well. We consider these proposals key for Europe to continue leading the climate and social agenda.

It is about identifying the areas of the energy transition with the greatest opportunities for job creation (renovation of buildings, renewables, storage of renewable energy, electrical mobility, biomethane, hydrogen) and going beyond the energy transition (the circular economy, the bioeconomy). It is also about identifying proposals to support companies better and driving plans in support of the transition in industry and other sectors.

Training for workers in the skills of the present and the future is an important part of our proposal. We must review the curricula of compulsory secondary education, professional training and university education, for the inclusion of ecological-transition contents.

Just-transition agreements

We must optimise the social gains of the ecological transition, but we also need without a doubt to mitigate the challenges. That is why, for those regions where the energy and ecological transition can put businesses and economic activity in difficulty, we have incorporated a tool for their revival—just-transition agreements, which must propose a comprehensive territorial action plan for them.

Just-transition agreements have as a priority objective the maintenance and creation of activity and employment in the region through working with the sectors and groups at risk, the maintenance of populations in rural territories in areas with installations facing closure and the promotion of a diversification and specialisation consistent with the socio-economic context.

In my first stint in charge of the Ministry for Ecological Transition, we had to face the closure of the Spanish mines and the request to close most of our coal-fired power plant. That is why we prepared an urgent action plan in which we committed ourselves to work together with all the administrations, the companies involved and the social actors on the transition agreements for these areas.

This plan arose from the agreement signed with the trade-union and business organisations for the closure of the mining sector, whose efforts were essential to advance the search for solutions. The agreement was associated with a strong, continuous dialogue with the mayors of the affected municipalities.

The agreements for these coal zones include numerous tools in support of investments, the restoration of the territories, support for industrial projects, the retraining of workers and the development of small and medium enterprises.

Also in a very innovative manner, at the end of 2019 we approved a regulation which allows us to put out to tender the network access and water use, of which coal-fired power plants avail themselves, to the best projects, not only in economic terms but also *vis-à-vis* employment generation. Two scarce resources in Spain, network access and water, are put at the service of job creation in the areas affected by closures, redirecting investments without the need to be supported with public resources—simply by approaching geographically opportunities and challenges, and taking into account the social benefits of these.

The preparation of the agreements is being carried out by means of participatory processes in which we propose an objective assessment of possible job losses and a commitment to a final list of projects born of the agreement between the parties, which will have to result in the maintenance of employment and population. This should represent a sustainable future project for these territories which were fundamental actors in generating the wealth of today—we have to recognise their contribution, respect their identity and help them to continue to be protagonists of the economic future of our country.

The just-transition agreements which have begun to develop must be signed with the territories which were living off coal in the coming months of May to October 2020. Fortunately, this proposal has generated important social support, demonstrated in the response to the various elections of the last year.

Finding a future

The population of the regions, although anxious and in many cases sceptical of the commitments made after a long restructuring which has been difficult and painful, is dedicated to finding a future for these territories and values honesty. Delaying debate or decision-making does not eliminate the problems—it simply leaves us in a worse position to solve them. Accelerating changes without putting people in the centre will equally have little traction and could lead to setbacks difficult to overcome.

As the priority of this new mandate of the Vice-Presidency for Ecological Transition and the Demographic Challenge, we have the opportunity to make a reality of our promises, demonstrating that social and climate ambition can go hand in hand and can also respect the wishes of the rural population fighting depopulation, in Spain and in the European Union as a whole.

THREE

THE ECONOMIC EFFECTS OF A PANDEMIC

SIMON WREN-LEWIS

A little over ten years ago I was approached by some health experts who wanted to look at the economic effects of an influenza pandemic. They needed someone with a macroeconomic model to look at the general equilibrium impacts. In the 1990s I had led a small team that constructed a model called COMPACT, and these health experts and I completed a paper that was subsequently published in *Health Economics*. We referenced other studies that had been done earlier in that paper.

The current coronavirus outbreak will have different characteristics to the pandemic we studied, and hopefully it will not become a pandemic at all. (In terms of mortality it seems to be somewhere in between the 'base case' and 'severe case' we looked at in our work.) But I think there were some general lessons from the exercise we did that will be relevant if this particular coronavirus does become a global pandemic. One proviso is that a key assumption we made about the pandemic is that it was mainly a three-month affair, and obviously what I have to say is dependent on it being short-lived.

The bottom line of all this for me is that the economics are secondary to the health consequences for any pandemic that has a significant fatality rate (as coronavirus so far appears to have). The economics are important in their own right and as a warning to avoid drastic measures that do not influence the number of deaths, but beyond that there is no meaningful trade-off between preventing deaths and losing some percentage of gross domestic product for less than half the year.

Least important

Let me start with the least important impact from an economic point of view, and that is the fall in production due to workers taking more time off sick. It is least important in part because firms have ways of compensating for this, particularly if illness is spread over the quarter. For example, those who have been sick and come back to work can work overtime. This will raise costs and might lead to some temporary inflation, but the central bank should ignore this.

This 'direct' impact of the pandemic in the UK will reduce GDP in that quarter by a few percentage points. The precise number will depend on what proportion of the population gets sick, on what the fatality rate turns out to be, and how many people miss work in an attempt not to get the disease. The impact on GDP for the whole year following the pandemic is much less at around 1 or 2 per cent, partly because output after the pandemic quarter is higher as firms replenish diminished stocks and meet postponed demand.

All this assumes schools do not close once the pandemic takes hold. School closures can amplify the reduction in labour supply if some workers are forced to take time off to look after children. On the basis of the assumptions we made, if schools close for around four weeks that can multiply the GDP impacts above by as much as a factor of three, and if they close for a whole quarter by twice that. If that seems large, remember nationwide school closures affect everyone with children and not just those with the disease.

But even with all schools closed for three months and many people avoiding work when they were not sick, the largest impact we got for GDP loss over a year was less than 5 per cent. That is a very severe one-quarter recession, but there is no reason why the economy cannot bounce back to full strength once the pandemic is over. Unlike a normal recession, information on the cause of the output loss, and therefore when it should end, is clear.

Demand shock

All this assumes that consumers who have not yet got the disease do not alter their behaviour. For a pandemic that spreads gradually this seems unlikely. The most important lesson I learnt from doing this study is that the pandemic need not just be a supply shock. It can also be a demand shock that can hit specific sectors very hard, depending on how consumers behave.

This is because a lot of our consumption nowadays can be called social, by which I mean doing things that bring you into contact with other people—things like going to the pub, to restaurants, to football matches or travel. Other sectors that provide consumption services that involve personal contact (such as haircuts) and can easily be postponed may also be hit.

If people start worrying about getting the disease sufficiently to cut back on this social consumption, the economic impact will be more severe than any numbers discussed so far. One reason it is severe is that it is partly a permanent loss. Maybe you will have a few more meals out once the pandemic is over to make up for what you missed when you stayed home, but there is likely to be a net fall in your consumption of meals out over the year. What I realised when I did the analysis was just how much of our consumption was social.

This is why the biggest impacts on GDP occur when we have people reducing their social consumption in an effort not to get the disease. However, falls in social consumption do not scale up all scenarios by the same amount, for the simple reason that supply and demand are complementary. If school closures and people taking more time off work increase the size of the supply shock, the demand shock has less scope to do damage. The largest fall in annual GDP in all the variants we looked at was 6 per cent.

Business closures

Could conventional monetary or fiscal policy offset the fall in social consumption? Only partially, because the drop in consumption is focused on specific sectors. What is more important, and what we didn't explore in the exercise, is what would happen if the banks failed to provide bridging finance for the firms having to deal with a sudden fall in demand. The banks may judge that some businesses that are already indebted may not be able to cope with any additional short-term loans, leading to business closures during the pandemic.

It is in this light that we should view the collapse of stock markets around the world. In macroeconomic terms this is a one-off shock, so Martin Sandbu is right that the recent stock market reaction looks overblown. But if many businesses are at financial risk from the temporary drop in social consumption, that implies a rise in the equity risk premia, which helps account for the size of the stock market collapse we have seen. (I say 'helps' deliberately, as much of the impact will be on smaller businesses that do not find their way into the main stock-market indices.)

If I was running the central bank or government, I would have already started having conversations with banks about not forcing firms into bankruptcy during any pandemic.

But economics can also influence health outcomes, and not just in terms of National Health Service resources. For a minority of self-employed workers there will be no sick pay and those without a financial cushion will be put under stress.

One of the concerns as far as the spread of the pandemic is concerned is that workers will not be able to afford to self-isolate if they have the disease. So if I was in government I would be thinking of setting up something like a sick-leave fund to which such workers could apply if they get coronavirus symptoms.

The government also needs to think about keeping public services and utilities running when workers in those services start falling ill. In fact there are a whole host of things the government should now be doing to prepare for a pandemic. It is at times like these that we really need governments to act fast and think ahead. Do we in the UK, and US citizens, have confidence that the government will do what is required? One lesson of coronavirus may be: never put into power politicians who have a habit of ignoring experts.

This first appeared on the author's Mainly Macro blog

FOUR

THE CORONA CRISIS WILL DEFINE OUR ERA

KARIN PETTERSSON

Mike Pence bowed his head in prayer. Around him in the White House, some of the world's most prominent scientists were gathered.

It was February 26th when the US vice-president and the scientists united in prayer, for—or, rather, against—the coronavirus epidemic. As governor of Indiana, Pence had made a name for himself driving drastic cuts in public-health funding and access to HIV-testing. This contributed to one of the largest outbreaks of the infection ever in his home state.

Since the 2016 elections, the administration of Donald Trump has slashed federal funding for pandemic prevention. The president has banned the country's leading experts from public comment. All communication is by way of Pence.

The pair are holding science to ransom. It is a profoundly degrading and depressing sight.

The question is how Trump's propaganda machine will deal with the situation if, or when, 200,000 Americans die from the virus? Will Fox News claim the infection was spread by immigrants?

The big one

This is the big one, this is the great crisis, the *Financial Times* writes. I am convinced that 2020 is a year that will define our era. One can compare it with the 2008 financial crisis. That led to recession and mass unemployment, but not to the death of hundreds of thousands.

In Sweden, the situation is getting more serious by the day, according to the Public Health Agency. But it inspires trust that the response is managed by experts, not by religious fanatics or politicians short-sightedly craving maximum public attention. And that management is being publicly scrutinised, questioned and discussed, as it should.

Yet this is still merely the beginning. First, the crisis arrives. Then comes the grief. Then comes the time for reflection.

Strong state

Already however, we know this: this type of disease cannot be efficiently fought at an individual level, but only as a society. It requires preparation, co-ordination, planning and the ability to make rapid decisions and scale up efforts. A strong state.

But nor is government enough. The situation demands personal responsibility, a sense of duty, concern for one's neighbour. If you do not belong to a risk group, your responsibility is not so much to protect yourself but to take care to protect others, even if that pushes you towards personal discomforts.

Yet what will you do if you simply cannot afford to stay at home? If you are illegally in Sweden (say), hiding from the authorities, or a 'gig' worker without regular salary in the US, living from hand to mouth? Sustaining health as a public good becomes impossible at a certain level of inequality and insecurity.

Bizarre times

This problem can be reduced neither to ethical virtues nor to a need for investments. What can be said, though, is that the crisis puts the flaws of our short-sighted, exploitative, hyper-individualistic times in glaring focus. Our bizarre era, where we pretend that we do not all connect, and that what *I* do does not actually affect *your* future.

At a global level we have underinvested for decades in research on infectious diseases and pandemics. Such investment does not produce fast profits and rising share prices for the medical companies, which much prefer to invest in research on heart disease, dealing with anxiety and erectile boosters. Public-health investments are not commercially viable in late capitalism.

This is just one example of the vulnerabilities we expose ourselves to. Economists call it 'market failure'. That expression says it all, really.

The 2008 financial crisis did not lead to any reassessment. Quite the contrary. No one knows what conclusions we will draw this time around, at an individual and collective level. I wonder if young people might come to think that authoritarian China dealt with the crisis better than the US—*the land of the free.*

Driving forces

I lie awake at night and various scenarios play out in my head. People in overcrowded hospital corridors, crashing stock markets. But, mostly, I think of my parents and friends in the risk group—people I immediately care about.

One cannot protect oneself against new diseases. What can be done is to mitigate and manage probable and possible events. The threat of pandemics—and the fact that we are quickly moving towards the so-called tipping points of the climate crisis—is well known. But the driving forces behind the short-sightedness of our economic and political system are so powerful that even known risks are impossible to manage.

The cash must keep flowing, quarter by quarter. Until the crash comes.

This article is a joint publication by Social Europe *and* IPS-Journal. *A Swedish version appeared in* Aftonbladet.

FIVE

THE FUTURE OF WORK IN THE POST-COVID-19 DIGITAL ERA

MARIA MEXI

The trend of working online from afar is experiencing a crucial boost, as Covid-19 compels companies and organisations to impose mandatory work-from-home policies in an increasingly 'no-touch' world. The sudden switch to remote digital work, overnight and *en masse,* has the potential to accelerate changes in how work is performed and the way we think about working arrangements.

Looking at the broader picture, Covid-19 may prove to be a major tipping point for the digital transformation of the workplace. It looks near impossible to put that digital genie back in the bottle, once the health emergency is over.

As the virus keeps spreading, some employees will be working from home—and in digitally-enabled environments not bound by a traditional office space—for the first time. Their working lives will be hugely disrupted and upturned. Yet, for millions of workers around the globe doing 'gig' work, moving their working lives online isn't new. It's just business as usual.

Especially for crowdworkers in the gig economy, 'work' is not a place: it is a web-based task or an activity, which can be done from any location that allows for internet connectivity. Many millennials and Generation Zers are living the gig-economy model today precisely for the flexibility and freedom remote digital work can offer. Covid-19 could be the catalyst which takes the evolution of 'work anywhere' arrangements to the next level of growth, in ways that considerably improve opportunities to collaborate, think, create and connect productively.

Huge strain

Not all is rosy, though. Currently, Covid-19 is putting the low-paid contingent of gig workers, often linked to digital platforms—such as ride-hailing and food delivery—under huge strain. After doctors, nurses and other healthcare workers, gig workers lacking any or adequate access to employment-insurance benefits or sick leave are the hardest hit in the United States, Europe and Asia. In countries with some of the biggest clusters of cases, such as Italy, some couriers working for food-delivery apps still go to work because they can't afford not to.

Thus, the Covid-19 crisis leaves especially those who depend on gig work as their primary source of income extremely vulnerable to (fatal) health risks. It undermines their dignity and it intensifies social and economic divides which may potentially generate new cleavages, anger and political discontent in countries and regions.

As the crisis evolves, gig workers won't be the only ones suffering even more than usual. The International Labour Organization published a 'high' global unemployment estimate of 24.7 million because of Covid-19 in mid-March; a week later, the head of its employment policy department warned the outcome could be 'far higher' still. By comparison, global unemployment increased by 22 million in the 2008-09 economic crisis. It is also expected that, worldwide, there could be as many as 35 million more in working poverty than before the pre-Covid-19 estimate for 2020.

Important message

These statistics send an important message: Protecting workers against the adverse impacts of the crisis is not only about increasing protection for typical jobs. It is also about including and protecting better those working at the margins: non-standard workers in tourism, travel, retail and other sectors most immediately affected, dependent self-employed persons with unstable incomes, zero-hours workers and low-paid workers in precarious working conditions who stand to gain little from the various countries' latest packages of emergency measures, as recent evidence shows.

Persistent gaps in social-protection coverage for workers—in 'old' and 'new' forms of employment—constitute a major challenge for our labour markets in the post-Covid-19 environment. This matters particularly for the future of the work we want to create in the digital era. We need to facilitate digital work, for the many benefits it can offer businesses and workers.

But we must not allow this to assume a form for workers—unprotected and socially deprived—too common in today's gig economy.

Next to the deadly human toll, the war metaphors which have been recently invoked by world leaders in the fight against Covid-19 reveal an uncomfortable truth. We are confronted with the flaws and fundamental weaknesses of our labour-market and social policies, solidarity mechanisms and models of collective responsibility for managing the risks that weigh unfairly and gravely on the most vulnerable citizens.

Decent digiwork

What can be done? A more expansive, resourceful and inclusive recovery is crucial, so that the impact of the Covid-19 crisis on labour markets becomes less far-reaching. We need to make our digital future immune to the 'virus' of precarity, with our labour markets built on the principle of human dignity and the potential of 'decent digiwork' for all.

This is a vision of full participation in a digital-work future which affords self-respect and dignity, security and equal opportunity, representation and voice. It is also about defining a 'digital responsibility by default' model—an entirely different mindset in society as to the role of governments and the private sector, in ensuring labour standards are updated to respond better to the evolving reality of digital workplaces.

In these tragic circumstances, there is a lesson for the future: the experience of gig workers shows going digital means more than just shifting channels. It is about refitting our labour markets, social-protection and welfare systems and making sure everyone has the ability to realise the human right to social security in the post-Covid-19 digital era. No society and no organised democracy can afford to ignore the vulnerable situations of workers who have few social protections yet are critical in a crisis.

Done right, we can shape a fair future of work. More than ever before therefore, the message for policy-makers, employers, workers and their representatives is straightforward: prepare for the next day. Bring precarious digital work into the realm of social protection. Take action for decent digiwork —now.

SIX

HOW HIS 'BREXIT' PROJECT EXPLAINS JOHNSON'S DITHERING ON COVID-19

PAUL MASON

On March 19th, even as its health service came under growing pressure from the coronavirus, the British government flatly refused to take part in a European Union joint-procurement scheme for vitally needed ventilators. The reasons are shrouded in obfuscation: the prime minister, Boris Johnson, first claimed the United Kingdom was going it alone 'because it has left the EU', but later he blamed an administrative error.

By then, the UK was two weeks into its disastrous 'herd immunity' strategy, whereby it refused to impose movement restrictions and—as we now know—spurned the mass testing advocated by the World Health Organization.

Some people have assumed that—as with the US president, Donald Trump, at the same stage—Johnson was prepared to sacrifice lives on a large scale to save the economy. But it's even simpler and more cruel than that. The entire month of February was wasted to save his 'Brexit' project.

Breaking commitments

Though Downing Street made no official announcement on the coronavirus until March 3rd, it was on Johnson's mind as a threat to Brexit exactly a month earlier. In a florid speech, set amid the splendour of Britain's 18th-century naval college in Greenwich, he announced the UK would effectively break the terms of the Political Declaration co-signed with the European Union in October 2019.

London would not honour its commitments to a 'level playing field', on social, environmental and employment regulations, and would not accept any form of joint jurisdiction, Johnson indicated. And if the EU didn't like it, preparations for a no-deal Brexit would begin as early as June.

Far from mirroring and matching the regulations of its closest trading bloc, the UK would now become a country single-handedly committed to breaking up all trading blocs, aggressively reordering world trade—just as during its naval sway in the days of Robert Clive and Horatio Nelson.

Public experiment

Most people missed it at the time, but the entire narrative was framed around a response to the coronoavirus.

'When there is a risk that new diseases such as coronavirus will trigger a panic and a desire for market segregation that go beyond what is medically rational to the point of doing real and unnecessary economic damage,' Johnson said, 'humanity needs some government somewhere that is willing at least to make the case powerfully for … the right of the populations of the earth to buy and sell freely among each other.'

The UK was to be that country. And, in the name of avoiding 'unnecessary economic damage', Johnson then subjected the entire British population to an experimental public health strategy which—until it was corrected on the advice of Imperial College researchers—might have killed a quarter of a million people.

While other European countries imposed legal population lockdowns, testing tens of thousands a day, Johnson's initial aim was to 'take it on the chin'—allowing 80 per cent of the population to catch the disease. He feared—rightly as it turns out—that Covid-19 would be yet another nail in the coffin of trade and financial globalisation, and thus the negation of the premise of his Brexit project.

Threat unsustainable

Though the 'herd immunity' strategy has been abandoned, so far Johnson is sticking to the threat of a no-deal Brexit.

Yet a glance at the realities of the world economy show that it is unsustainable. Numerous 'sudden stops' are under way, both on the demand and supply sides of the real economy. In response there is capital flight from two key sectors: emerging markets and developed-country commercial paper. And as investors scramble for short-dated government debt, as a cash equivalent, even the market for government bonds has been in turmoil.

According to the ratings agency Fitch, it is likely that global gross domestic product will fall by 1.9 per cent for the whole of 2020, with the UK and the eurozone seeing year-on-year declines of 3.3 and 4.2 per cent respectively. And these projections are being made before we know the extent of any secondary financial aftershocks.

The best-case scenario is a V-shaped recession, with GDP back to its pre-crisis levels only in late 2021. If central banks and treasuries cannot stave off financial chaos, a longer, U-shaped recession becomes likely. If, on top of that, austerity-addicted politicians decide to attack wages and public spending in the budget rounds of 2021, it is possible parts of the world will experience a Greek-style, L-shaped recession, during which some governments go bust.

Illusion shattered

In this context, proceeding with the December 2020 deadline —and the threat of a no-deal Brexit to be triggered in June— is self-destructive. But then again so was the refusal to collaborate on procuring medical supplies, and so was the 'herd immunity' strategy.

Johnson had convinced himself that—by disruptively leaving the single 'market—he could set a chain reaction going against the rise of protectionism and the emergence of trading blocs. Just two months later, that illusion has been shattered. The coronavirus has, if anything, accelerated the deglobalisation of the world which began after 2008.

At a purely physical level, given the likelihood that the virus will recirculate in waves for years, international travel is likely to be disrupted. As major powers scramble for the industrial capacity to produce ventilators, masks, tests and vaccines, there are calls everywhere for the creation of more secure and reliable local supply chains.

The same goes for food: the panic buying which swept the developed world's supermarkets in March reflected the rational fear of people at the end of global supply chains that these might break, or be vulnerable to political disruption, as the virus spreads to the food-producing regions of the world.

And the next deglobalisation will be of finance. Up to now the fiscal stimulus unleashed by many countries has failed to show up in deficit figures and debt projections. In the UK's case it is hard to see anything smaller than £200 billion being added to public debt. In the USA, Wells Fargo estimates the crisis will enhance the federal debt by $2.8 trillion. As for the eurozone, the final figure depends on whether the peripheral countries overcome the resistance of Germany and the Netherlands to debt mutualisation.

Qualitative change

Once we emerge from this recession, the world will have changed in a qualitative way. The combined government debts of the G7 countries will be way above their pre-crisis average of 118 per cent of GDP. Some central banks will have begun to 'monetise' those debts—buying gilts directly from their treasuries—thereby placing pressure on the free flow of capital across borders, and on some currencies.

For Britain voluntarily to trigger a no-deal crisis in this situation would be madness. Even the emergency supplies which ministers take delight in personally delivering in front of the cameras are drawn from stockpiles amassed in preparation for a no-deal Brexit.

The absence of global leadership and co-ordination amid the coronavirus crisis signals that the exit from it may be competitive, insular and in some cases autarkic.

China is using its early recovery to pursue overt diplomatic and trade leverage with countries signed up to its Belt and Road Initiative. Russia is using the crisis to attempt to destabilise eastern Europe, its state media continually blaring the message that the EU is collapsing. The United States, which has unleashed the biggest and most direct fiscal stimulus, and whose central bank is for now playing a global leadership role, is simultaneously engaged in a medical supply-chain land grab, using every ounce of its geopolitical muscle.

Project dead

Domestically, Johnson's project is already dead. The whole point of hard Brexit was to deregulate the labour market and reduce social protections and environmental standards, while scapegoating 'migrants' and 'Europe' for everything that went wrong. It is not clear whether, in the aftermath of the crisis, Johnson will even survive the inevitable public inquiry into the decisions made.

As for the Greenwich speech, the world it was made in has disappeared. It was always an illusion that the UK could somehow kickstart a second wave of globalisation on its own. Realistically, it might have done so as the sidekick to a US government similarly inclined. But Trump wants to do the opposite—and it is hard to see any US president emerging from the trauma of the epidemic with the willpower to revive an open, multilateral global order.

The UK Treasury has given up trying to predict the negative economic effects of a hard Brexit: its guidance to its own fore-casters at the Office for Budget Responsibility at the March budget was perfunctory. In November 2018, however, it predicted that, 15 years after a hard Brexit, Britain's GDP would be 9.3 per cent lower than if it had stayed in the EU. The short-term effect of no deal, modelled around the same time by the Bank of England, was a drop in output of 3 to 7 per cent in a single year.

Even by a crude process of addition—let alone the multiplier effects of consecutive crises—it is obvious that a hard Brexit on December 31st could turn a sharp, six-month recession into a two-to-three-year slump.

Labour's task

Keir Starmer, who now assumes control of the Labour Party, knows the hard Brexit project was always designed as a political trap. If he acts in the interests of the country and the electorate, by insisting on a deal which maintains a level playing field with access to the single market, Labour will be pilloried for 'sabotaging Brexit'. Yet if he calls for a one-year delay, yet again the right-wing rhetoric of 'betrayal' will be deployed.

Starmer has said that rejoining the EU is off the agenda for the foreseeable future. Given his strategic task is to reconnect the party with communities where there is deep xenophobia and Euroscepticism, that is sensible.

But in a world order facing disintegration, geographical facts prevail. The EU is the UK's main trading partner; after nearly half a century of participation, European integration is imprinted on its laws, customs and culture; and, as the world becomes insecure, its security relies on the security of Europe. So long as the EU coheres as a single market, Britain's safest place is within its orbit.

Starmer's internal critics, on the socially conservative 'blue Labour' wing and on the economic-nationalist left, want the party to forget about Brexit. Unfortunately that's not possible.

Labour needs to call immediately for a one-year delay to Brexit, and for the repudiation of the UK's February 2020 negotiating document, in favour of a comprehensive trade agreement leaving it in close partnership with the EU, while keeping migration as open as possible.

Finally, it is worth noting the difference between the UK's global role today and that which it played in 2008. The then prime minister, Gordon Brown, convened a G20 summit which produced real and lasting post-crisis co-ordination, both of stimulus and regulation. Johnson may have luxuriated beneath the Greenwich murals depicting Britain's former greatness, but Brown actually did something.

And that is the final part of the critique Labour must put in place: a global fiscal stimulus, monetary co-ordination and a transnational industrial mobilisation are all essential to beat this virus.

This article is a joint publication by Social Europe *and* IPS-Journal

SEVEN

CAPITALISM'S TRIPLE CRISIS

MARIANA MAZZUCATO

Capitalism is facing at least three major crises. A pandemic-induced health crisis has rapidly ignited an economic crisis with yet unknown consequences for financial stability, and all of this is playing out against the backdrop of a climate crisis that cannot be addressed by 'business as usual'. Until just two months ago, the news media were full of frightening images of overwhelmed firefighters, not overwhelmed health-care providers.

This triple crisis has revealed several problems with how we do capitalism, all of which must be solved at the same time that we address the immediate health emergency. Otherwise, we will simply be solving problems in one place while creating new ones elsewhere. That is what happened with the 2008 financial crisis. Policy-makers flooded the world with liquidity without directing it toward good investment opportunities. As a result, the money ended up back in a financial sector that was (and remains) unfit for purpose

The Covid-19 crisis is exposing still more flaws in our economic structures, not least the increasing precarity of work, owing to the rise of the gig economy and a decades-long deterioration of workers' bargaining power. Telecommuting simply is not an option for most workers and, although governments are extending some assistance to workers with regular contracts, the self-employed may find themselves left high and dry.

Worse, governments are now extending loans to businesses at a time when private debt is already historically high. In the United States, total household debt just before the current crisis was $14.15 trillion, which is $1.5 trillion higher than it was in 2008 (in nominal terms). And, lest we forget, it was high private debt that caused the global financial crisis.

Unfortunately, over the past decade, many countries have pursued austerity, as if public debt were the problem. The result has been to erode the very public-sector institutions that we need to overcome crises like the coronavirus pandemic.

Since 2015, the United Kingdom has cut public-health budgets by £1 billion, increasing the burden on doctors in training (many of whom have left the National Health Service altogether), and reducing the long-term investments needed to ensure that patients are treated in safe, up-to-date, fully staffed facilities. And in the US—which has never had a properly funded public-health system—the Trump administration has been persistently trying to cut funding and capacity for the

Centers for Disease Control and Prevention, among other critical institutions.

On top of these self-inflicted wounds, an overly 'financialised' business sector has been siphoning value out of the economy by rewarding shareholders through stock-buyback schemes, rather than shoring up long-run growth by investing in research and development, wages and worker training. As a result, households have been depleted of financial cushions, making it harder to afford basic goods like housing and education.

Inclusive and sustainable

The bad news is that the Covid-19 crisis is exacerbating all these problems. The good news is that we can use the current state of emergency to start building a more inclusive and sustainable economy. The point is not to delay or block government support, but to structure it properly. We must avoid the mistakes of the post-2008 era, when bailouts allowed corporations to reap even higher profits once the crisis was over but failed to lay the foundation for a robust and inclusive recovery.

This time, rescue measures absolutely must come with conditions attached. Now that the state is back to playing a leading role, it must be cast as the hero rather than as a naive patsy. That means delivering immediate solutions, but designing them in such a way as to serve the public interest over the long term.

For example, conditionalities can be put in place for government support to businesses. Firms receiving bailouts should be asked to retain workers, and ensure that once the crisis is over they will invest in worker training and improved working conditions. Better still, as in Denmark, government should be supporting businesses to continue paying wages even when workers are not working—simultaneously helping households to retain their incomes, preventing the virus from spreading and making it easier for businesses to resume production once the crisis is over.

Moreover, bailouts should be designed to steer larger companies to reward value creation instead of value extraction, preventing share buybacks and encouraging investment in sustainable growth and a reduced carbon footprint.
Having declared last year that it will embrace a stakeholder-value model, this is the Business Roundtable's chance to back its words with action. If corporate America is still dragging its feet now, we should call its bluff.

When it comes to households, governments should look beyond loans to the possibility of debt relief, especially given current high levels of private debt. At a minimum, creditor payments should be frozen until the immediate economic crisis is resolved and direct cash injections used for those households that are in direst need. And the US should offer government guarantees to pay 80-100 per cent of distressed companies' wage bills, as the UK and many European Union and Asian countries have done.

Parasitic arrangements

It is also time to rethink public-private partnerships. Too often, these arrangements are less symbiotic than parasitic. The effort to develop a Covid-19 vaccine could become yet another one-way relationship, in which corporations reap massive profits by selling back to the public a product that was born of taxpayer-funded research. Indeed, despite US taxpayers' significant public investment in vaccine development, the US secretary of health and human services, Alex Azar, recently conceded that newly developed Covid-19 treatments or vaccines might not be affordable to all Americans.

We desperately need entrepreneurial states that will invest more in innovation—from artificial intelligence to public health to renewables. But as this crisis reminds us, we also need states that know how to negotiate, so that the benefits of public investment return to the public.

A killer virus has exposed major weaknesses within western capitalist economies. Now that governments are on a war footing, we have an opportunity to fix the system. If we don't, we will stand no chance against the third major crisis—an increasingly uninhabitable planet—and all the smaller crises that will come with it in the years and decades ahead.

Republication forbidden—copyright Project Syndicate 2020, 'Capitalism's triple crisis'

SOLIDARISTIC, SOCIAL AND SENSIBLE —REFLECTIONS ON PROGRESSIVISM FOR TODAY AND WHEN TOMORROW COMES

ANIA SKRZYPEK

The coronavirus crisis is a profoundly transformative experience. Hardly anyone (outside of epidemiologists) had predicted the catastrophe coming the way it did.

Thousands of pages had been written about globalisation and modernity. A great many featured terrifying, doomsday scenarios. But what has happened has gone beyond anything ever imagined. Now there is no way of knowing how long this will all take, how many lives will be claimed and what kind of world will emerge.

So resorting to comfortable intellectual templates by way of explanation would prove treacherous. It is time humbly to admit that not only will the world be different—and it will simply be impossible to pick up where we left off—but also it isn't an option to revisit essays on previous crises and replace 'economic' with 'coronavirus'. Never before has the saying 'the future is unknown' been more true.

Put to the test

If there is therefore a need to turn the page, there is also a need to understand what this confinement has done to ordinary lives. It has put individuals to the test. They have had to revise what they consider essential and inessential, in both materialistic and non-materialistic senses.

It has put households too to the test, making individuals acquire a new closeness by default. Those within confinement together have had to learn a great deal about one another, while those at a distance have started communicating more frequently. Some perhaps have never called their parents and grandparents as often as during these days.

Moreover, a new kind of responsibility has been emerging within communities, whereby the younger would volunteer to bring groceries or go to the pharmacy for those elders, the first to be advised to stay home. And the courage and devotion of so many has made others realise superheroes live among them. These are not only the doctors and nurses but also the shop assistant in the grocery around the corner, the teacher from the nursery that wasn't closed to provide care for those ensuring continuity of vital services, the refuse collector, the post-office clerks, the lorry drivers …

With white flags hung on so many buildings and at 8 pm people opening their windows to cheer and applaud, a sense of gratitude, solidarity and a new admiration for others has been born. Paradoxically then, people may feel themselves closer as a result of the lockdown—more connected and more respectful towards other—than they have been in decades. This would, if sustained, be a reversal of years of atomisation of contemporary societies.

Issues foregrounded

Furthermore, confinement foregrounded issues that had been known and talked about at length, for at least two decades, but had not been given the priority they should. Appropriate elderly care, alongside the need to invest more and equip adequately institutions providing healthcare, is evidently top of the list. But it includes many other, less obvious, matters.

Lockdown left many imprisoned, alone, within their own houses, questioning the adequacy of existing support mechanisms. For the impoverished, it raised again the question of what minimum standards are, especially when shops had to limit their offer to essential goods. The tragedy also exposed the absolute necessity to do more to fight children's poverty, as nobody could guarantee during the lockdown that each and every child had even one warm meal a day.

Mental health and care for patients suffering from chronic disease—for whom human contact has a therapeutic relevance and who were from one day to another left to a potential decline—were also at issue. As was the quest to fight domestic violence: it pains even to think how much more suffering there has been in conditions of confinement. Finally, the continuing lack of provision in many places for same-sex marriage presented an incredibly cruel obstacle to partners remaining together in challenging moments in hospitals and elsewhere.

Managing to adapt

The new life brought on many challenges. And, although it all happened under immense pressure, it has been quite extraordinary to see how quickly and brilliantly people managed to adapt. The already oft-posed question 'How will people manage in the era of digitalisation?' received particularly rapidly replies.

Some, such as teleconferencing or sharing data, were merely intensifications, but alongside them came fresh inventions. Teleworking prompted many employers to negotiate the rules and set guidelines. Virtual classrooms and e-lessons made teachers and students acquire new skills, as also due to necessity many parents and guardians became much more aware about the content of their children's education. Even gyms and other social institutions found e-solutions—proving yet again that no matter how virtual, the human need to connect with others remains vital.

While acknowledging this creativity and perseverance, not all sectors could find sustainable solutions. Many people entered a precarious situation of at least temporary unemployment with, in some cases, no income whatsoever. On the back of that, some controversial debates returned—for example, on a universal basic income, though this represented an elision of a minimum-income guarantee. Refraining for the moment from arguing in favour or against, it is quite clear that once again the economic system as it is is in no way crash-proofed.

Future of social democracy

How then does this translate into the debate on the future of social democracy? While the coronavirus crisis is a hard test of leadership, in its aftermath citizens will come up with a new set of expectations, to which progressives should be able to relate.

First, the catastrophe has been directly felt by everyone. It wasn't just something to read about in the news and it wasn't anything from which one could distance oneself. Interpersonal connections forged and strengthened during the lockdown will naturally weaken after, but they will not disappear. The feeling of 'being in it together', the awareness about each other's needs, the mutual respect and admiration for those who helped get us through these times, is likely to be here to stay.

The prospect of new, solidaristic communities emerging is thus quite real and can provide a counter-current to the neoliberal tide of atomisation. Especially so since staying in touch was made possible thanks to the same internet tools and applications previously considered solvents of face-to-face human relations.

So while progressives of course would not have wished for such disastrous circumstances, these new collectives may be what they had been hoping to see. The speech of the 'strong political actor' will not however connect with them. Neither will an articulation of a list of complaints about the shortcomings of different institutions. What could, on the other hand, is social democracy finding it in itself to be the most humane, empathic movement—pretty much in the way Jacinda Ardern in New Zealand (where the virus has been successfully contained) is trying to do that. In the long term this can be a shield against the negativism of the right-wingers as well.

Secondly, the crisis has shown that people can actually quite quickly start to think in a totally different way. Before, patriotism was a term evoking association with national pride. Today, it has become identified with taking responsibility for others and recognising societal demands. So though the connecting points and building blocks of a new, post-catastrophe, majority-winning political agenda cannot be fully defined yet, there is no doubt it is going to be driven by social issues.

A new narrative

Yes, it will still revolve around the fight against inequalities. But it cannot be a recycled blueprint or anything that would remotely claim 'this is what we have been saying all the time'. The next challenge is most probably an incomparable economic crash and recession, which will demand a new narrative, reflecting a shift in thinking.

Before the crisis, it was legitimate to speak about the ambition of a new enlightenment. Now the mission should rather be *a new renaissance*—which in its hopes, its uplifting story of progress, its openness and attractiveness, with humanist values at its core, could break through in these dark times of inquisitional far-right figures who want still to spread fear. When tomorrow comes, people are likely not to be driven by anger or anxiety, but to be seeking something positive. They may be motivated rather by a desire to do the utmost to insure themselves against anything like the situation at hand—collectively and individually.

Thirdly and finally, while the pandemic has been the possibly toughest experience in Europe since the collapse of former Yugoslavia, it has also been the ultimate test of political leadership across the world. And the evaluation criteria have changed. Today what seems to define a true leader is his or her capabilities to provide stability, care and truth.

This is a remarkable turning point: people locked at home, relying on the internet themselves, want better than misinformation. They want to know *the truth, the whole truth and nothing but the truth*—that, while they follow emergency rules, they retain their right to self-determination and that what is being done is in their vital interest.

This is also why the behaviour of populists such as Viktor Orbán, Jarosław Kaczyński or Boris Johnson must finally be met with contempt. There is a real chance that instead citizens will confide in those, such as the Spanish, Czech and Danish social-democratic leaders—Pedro Sanchez, Jan Hamáček and Mette Frederiksen respectively—who emerge as responsible, caring and solution-driven.

NINE

OUT OF THE TRAGEDY OF CORONAVIRUS MAY COME HOPE OF A MORE JUST SOCIETY

MICHAEL D HIGGINS

The global loss of life and disruption to our daily lives resulting from the coronavirus pandemic is unprecedented in living memory. We have learned through tragedy that we have a shared, globalised vulnerability common to all humanity. We are learning how we, as a matter of urgency, must make changes to improve resilience in a range of essential areas: employment, healthcare, housing. We have been forced to recognise our dependence on our public-sector frontline workers, and the state's broader role in mitigating this crisis and saving lives.

The coronavirus has magnified the scale of our existing social crises and has proved, if ever proof were required, how government can act decisively when the will is there. It has shown us how so many are only ever one wage payment away from impoverishment, how those in self-employment or workers in the 'gig' economy lack security and basic employment rights, how private tenants in unregulated housing markets are at the mercy of their landlords, how many designated 'key workers' are appallingly undervalued and underpaid. Averting our gaze to these grim truths is no longer an option.

Years of eroding welfare states in many societies have had to give way, under pressure from the virus, to significant welfare actions as emergency measures. These reflect the impact decades of unfettered neoliberalism have had on whole sectors of society and economy, left without protection as to basic necessities of life, security and the ability to participate.

Widespread recognition

There is now a widespread, recovered recognition not only of the state's positive role in managing such crises but of how it can play a decisive, transformative role in our lives for the better. The erosion of the state's role, the weakening of its institutions and the undermining of its significance for over four decades has left us with a less just and more precarious society and economy.

As we respond, and thinking of the labour market, there is no precedent for the asymmetric mix of mobilisation and demobilisation of labour we are now witnessing. Writing in *Social Europe* recently, Jan Zielonka astutely remarked:

> [T]he coronavirus has exposed the scale of the public
> sector's neglect after a long period of neoliberal folly.
> Today no one in Europe dares to claim that private
> hospitals can combat the virus better than the public
> ones. Underpaid nurses from these public hospitals are
> now more precious than private health consultants.

How regrettable it is that it has taken a pandemic in which thousands of lives have been lost in so many countries to establish, or rekindle, widespread appreciation of work in the public sphere, of the public sector and the importance in the economy of the public good—and, in terms of our shared future, the state's benign and transformative capacity.

Many concerned citizens had hoped, even mistakenly believed, that progressive political-economy paradigms would flow from the 2008 financial crash. As the 'free-market' economist Milton Friedman correctly identified in *Capitalism and Freedom*, 'Only a crisis—actual or perceived—produces real change … When that crisis occurs, the actions that are taken depend on the ideas that are lying around.'

New ideas are now required—ideas based on equality, universal public services, equity of access, sufficiency, sustainability. New ideas are available for an alternative paradigm of social economy within ecological responsibility.

Fortunately, we now have a richer discourse, thanks to scholars such as Ian Gough, Mariana Mazzucato, Sylvia Walby, Kate

Raworth and others who advance an ecologically sustainable and socially progressive alternative to our destructive, failed paradigm.

Mazzucato has recently proposed that any firm-level financial assistance provided to recapitalise major companies should be conditional on a 'greening' agenda for its receipt. Such a suggestion is a useful contribution as we forge ahead with an eco-social paradigm which now represents our best hope for a sustainable future.

Brighter horizon

Out of respect for those who have suffered greatly, those who have lost their lives and indeed the bereaved families, we must not drift into some notion that we can recover what we had previously as a sufficient resolution—that we can revert to the insecurity of where we were before, through mere adjustment of fiscal- and monetary-policy parameters. That would be so wholly insufficient to the task now at hand. A brighter horizon must be put forward which offers hope.

The coronavirus provides us with an opportunity to do things better. This crisis will pass, but there will be other viruses and other crises. We cannot let ourselves be left in the same vulnerable position again. We have, yet again, learned lessons in relation to healthcare and equity, in relation to what is necessary in terms of income and the necessities of life.

On the most basic level, we should recover and strengthen instincts which we may have suppressed, which the lure of individualism may have driven out, displacing a sense of the collective, of shared solidarity—allowing the state's value and contribution to be derided and disregarded, so that a narrow agenda of accumulation could be pursued.

The coronavirus has highlighted the unequivocal case for a new eco-social political economy—of having universal basic services that will protect us in the future, as Anna Coote and Andrew Percy have suggested, and of enabling people to have a sufficiency of what they need, as Ian Gough has contended.

We also need, as is now urgent and as Oxfam's recent report shows, global solidarity if we are to avoid healthcare collapse in many developing countries, including in sub-Saharan Africa. We require enhanced attempts at the global level to build a new international architecture, to reverse the policy of fragmentation and institutional damage that has in recent years affected the United Nations and other multilateral organisations.

Transformative actions

Transformative actions are required. The recently published, meticulously researched analysis by Ireland's National Economic and Social Council (NESC) of the 'just transition' is a seminal document, offering a useful intellectual framework for the wider challenge we face as we attempt to forge a new path to an enlightened political economy, founded on ecology, social cohesion and equality. That report recommends a 'purposeful, participative and multi-faceted approach to governance; appropriate social protection for those at risk from transition impacts; supportive arrangements and sectoral measures, and inclusive place-based development and investment'.

I support NESC's call for the establishment of a social dialogue and deliberative process, which should be framed in the wider context of discussions as to how we embed the just economy and society now so urgently needed and desired by the citizenry.

Successful crisis management is no guarantee of durable reform. We therefore need to embed the hard-earned wisdom from this crisis into strong scholarly work, policy and institutional frameworks—this is the great challenge from a political-economy perspective. It will require, as NESC identifies, determined action by all governments, setting out priority actions, the sequence of interventions and timeframes for implementation, as well as consideration of what resources are needed.

Understandably, much current economic commentary focuses on the cost of the pandemic, but we must also reflect on the systemic weaknesses it has exposed in how we organise our society and economy. How can we address these frailties? How can we do things better, to realise the paradigm shift that is urgently required?

Our challenge is therefore to draw on the lessons of solidarity and ingenuity as the coronavirus confronts 21st-century society and its world economy with a new kind of emergency hazard —galvanising that sentiment across the citizenries of the globe which recognises the inherent flaws of our current model, and embracing a new paradigm founded on universalism, sustainability and equality.

What is a further, real basis for hope is that, within such a framework, it is possible to respond together to the coronavirus, climate change, the impact of digitalisation and an inequality which threatens democracy itself.

TEN

FOUR SCENARIOS FOR EUROPE'S FUTURE AFTER THE CRISIS

PHILIPPE POCHET

It's now clear the Covid-19 pandemic will have major, long-term consequences. In the European Union, the very foundations of European integration are being questioned.

The EU is defined by its 'pillars': the single market and free movement, the euro and the Stability and Growth Pact, and competition and state-aid law. These three pillars are being shaken by the pandemic and they are sure to be at the centre of debates on the future of Europe.

National borders

As regards the free movement of people, the closing once more of national borders has been a highly symbolic trend, demonstrating that 'other' Europeans are still considered as potentially dangerous, disease-carrying foreigners. This poses very delicate questions. When and under what conditions (health, economic, political) will a reopening be considered—without engendering too much risk? And at what scale—the Schengen area or groups of countries with similar risk levels (Benelux, the Baltic states, the Iberian peninsula), as the European Commission seems to be suggesting?

In the absence of a common approach to managing the health crisis, most likely will be the persistence of more or less tight internal borders for a long time. As for the EU's external borders, the example of China suggests strict 'cocooning' of the national territory *vis-à-vis* the outside world, having overcome the internal health crisis, is set to be the norm.

In the context of a monetary union devoid of solidarity mechanisms and without supranational political governance, the rules of the Stability and Growth Pact have been (temporarily) suspended—in sharp contrast to the eurozone crisis. But, here again, what will happen after? There are different ways of financing budget deficits and state debts, which are bound to explode. The consequences of these seemingly technical choices vary greatly in terms of their fiscal and, manifestly, social impact. Whether we resort to 'helicopter' money or 'coronabonds' or stick to the European Stability Mechanism —how the recovery is financed and what type of recovery it is —will greatly affect the future.

Moreover, are the institutional innovations being adopted temporary or longer-term—is the SURE initiative (supporting short-time work arrangements) the beginning of an EU unemployment-reinsurance system? And while the previous crisis did not allow of any progress towards the supranational governance of the currency, this one will be the last opportunity to do so.

Finally, the relaxation of state-aid restrictions and the rescue of companies in distress will reconfigure what is considered possible and legitimate. At stake is the legitimacy of the state to intervene in economic life. The effects of this crisis on the real economy will last for a long time, meaning that Europe will not soon get back to normal.

This in turn allows different choices from before. Will the role of the state in the economy, whether direct or indirect, be focused on 'rescuing' traditional sectors (air transport, oil or vehicle production) or will it be to push us towards an ecological transformation?

Different foundations

The post-crisis EU—assuming it survives—could have very different foundations if the questioning of the three pillars continues. But in which global environment is this set to happen? There are four possible scenarios.

The first (contrary to what I have written before) is a possible return to neoliberal orthodoxy—a bit like the previous crisis (2008-13), when Europe reverted even more radically to neoliberal fundamentals after a more or less green recovery in 2009. This was what eminent researchers have called the strange non-death of neoliberalism. This scenario is unlikely this time but not to be ruled out.

True, it's difficult to see austerity being applied to the public sector in one or two years' time. Yet the reactions of certain national employer organisations, growing tensions within certain states (and the conflict in the United States between governors and the president) and the bailouts of industrial and service sectors without real social or environmental conditions point in this direction.

The second scenario is the Chinese path, under which we move towards a more authoritarian state monitoring a country's population via new means based on artificial intelligence, with restrictions put on sometimes quite fundamental freedoms in exchange for a feeling of protection (purportedly of the country's territory). The fact that this health crisis could be recurrent opens up possibilities for more authoritarian governments, such as in Hungary and Poland, to assert themselves as the guarantors of their citizens' safety and security.

This scenario goes hand-in-hand with global fragmentation and a more or less radical 'deglobalisation'. Here again, the example of the US under Donald Trump, above all with the possibility of a second term, is telling. The relevant unit becomes the national territory—with social control ramped up with the help of 5G networks.

Growth at any price

The third scenario is a return to growth at any price, with unfettered catch-up consumption without any consideration for the environment. Reminiscent of the *Belle Époque*, this would be nothing less than an end-of-the-world party. While it would obviously have a positive impact on conventional economic indicators (such as gross domestic product) and would reduce bankruptcies and unemployment in the short and medium term, it would have major long-term consequences.

The calls of certain governments, such as in the Czech Republic, and sectoral actors to forget the European Green Deal underline the strength of this scenario. And should consumption not really pick up again, calls for recovery would give new impetus to demands for less account to be taken of environmental concerns and for greater labour-market 'flexibility' at the expense of workers. Seen this way, the third scenario could greatly resemble the first.

The final scenario involves accelerating the ecological transition and rapidly rethinking our growth model, with a return to public services, common goods and solidarity at the heart of the economy and social affairs. We are seeing the seeds of this, with several governments and civil-society players supporting the Green Deal and certain cities, such as Paris and Brussels, showing the way to a faster transition—albeit one very difficult to complete amid high unemployment and economic crisis.

Two factors are set to have a decisive influence. The first is the partial relocation of production chains and a certain environmental protectionism, which *in extremis* could have a lot in common with the second, nationalistic scenario. The key question would be whether co-operative protectionism (aimed at achieving the same goal) rather than antagonistic protectionism (winning against others) gained the upper hand.

The second and key factor is reduction of working time. It constitutes a dividing line between the neoliberal restoration and this recovery-at-all-costs scenario and comprises a strategic tipping-point. In my view it is strategically the most important aspect in structuring upcoming debates.

These scenarios are not mutually exclusive and can be combined and developed in parallel in different regions of the world, depending on the relevant balance of power. It might only take a little to switch from one to another. The strategy of collective actors will therefore play a key role—with consequences for the way the architectural pillars of the EU are transformed.

LIST OF AUTHORS

Gabriel Zucman is associate professor of economics at UC Berkeley. He is the author of *The Triumph of Injustice: How the Rich Dodge Taxes and How to Make Them Pay*.

Teresa Ribera is deputy prime minister for the ecological transition and the demographic challenge in Spain.

Simon Wren-Lewis is Professor of Economics at Oxford University.

Karin Pettersson is culture editor at *Aftonbladet*, Scandinavia's biggest daily newspaper. She founded *Fokus*, Sweden's leading news magazine, and worked for the Swedish Social Democratic Party.

Dr Maria Mexi is a consultant at the International Labour Organization and affiliated with the Albert Hirschman Centre of Democracy, the University of Geneva Political Science Department and the United Nations Research Institute for Social Development.

Paul Mason is a leading British writer and broadcaster and author of *Postcapitalism: A Guide to Our Future*.

Mariana Mazzucato is professor of the economics of innovation and public value and director of the University College London Institute for Innovation and Public Purpose.

Ania Skrzypek is director of research and training at the Foundation for European Progressive Studies.

Michael D Higgins is the ninth president of Ireland.

Philippe Pochet is general director of the European Trade Union Institute (ETUI). He is author of *À la recherche de l'Europe sociale* (ETUI, 2019).